I0094696

Shattered Glass

Richard White

First Printing 2019
Ingramspark Edition
ISBN-13: 978-0-578-49605-4

Personal Message

CONTENTS

CONTENTS

II Broken Glass   **35**

III Compass of Light   51

IV Shattered   69

V Random Thoughts — 81

VI Spoken Word   99

In Memory

Sometimes we find a path in our lives that is just not what we had in mind. Many of us including myself went down this path, some have survived, some are barely surviving, and some never made it into the clearing. Those of us that survived, wonder why we couldn't or didn't reach the ones that didn't make it out of the turmoil, and lost their lives because of it. This is my testament to that darkness that I face every day. The time from my past that at one point was so dark, no one could reach me. I found my way out with a broken compass, and a map with no lines or highways.

This book of poetry is in memory of those we have lost from high school, so many taken from us way to soon, because they lost their battle with drugs, and depression. They couldn't find the good in life, and chose a way out, that we survivors will never truly understand.

In particular Shattered glass is in memoriam of Jordan Bemis, he had such a gentle soul, and was a remarkable man, yet the demons overcame him, and he lost his battle, we miss him every day, and the more fellow students we lose from Mill River Union High School, the more we miss him, and the many others that we have lost.

It is my hope, that reading this book you find something in it that will help you find the good in life, and proceed to do battle with these demons, as I do.

Rekindling friendships from my class has been the best thing that I could ever do. This book is for them; Class of 98, thank you for being my friend.

Dear Reader,

The poetry in this book reflects my own darkness, how I deal with it, how the darkness makes me feel, and what it does to my mind, body and soul.

The point of this book is not to trigger you, but also show you how I healed myself from being broken. You don't have to be defined by your pain, and suffering, you can find a way to overcome the darkness, tragedies, and turmoil. I truly believe in this, and I believe in you. If this book does help change things for your darkness, feel free to contact me about how it changed your life.

If this book touches your triggers, and you need help please contact someone immediately.

National Suicide Prevention Hotline
1-800-273-8255
https://suicidepreventionlifeline.org/

Substance Abuse Mental Health Services
Administration
SAMHSA's National Helpline, 1-800-662-HELP
(4357)
https://www.samhsa.gov

The National Alliance on Mental Illness (NAMI)
Helpline,
https://www.nami.org
(800) 950-NAMI (6264); or text NAMI to 741741:

DEDICATION

This book takes me back to the roots of my writing. I started with poetry twenty years ago and traveled off into many places with my writing. However, I have returned to the subtle sonnets and rhythm of poetry because of the truth, love, passion, and feeling it can convey. I could do this because of a dear friend I have. Without meeting her and reading her work, I wouldn't remember how much I love poetry. I dedicate this book to her, Anais Chartschenko, for helping me discover that no matter where my writing leads me, I still have a love for verse. Her writing, made me feel like I once felt as I first wrote in my first journal. Nothing has brought me to that somber feeling, yet when I pick up her books, and read such passion, fear, and love, it makes the hair stand up on the back of my neck. I hope that as you read this book; you feel that same feeling. The darkness has come over me for so many years. I can channel it through words and get the relief that things don't have to be that dark anymore. When you read my poetry or any of my work, my one true goal is to pass that feeling on to you as a reader. That when things get dark, and the gloom settles in, there is a hope that one day you will not have to feel that darkness, and you too will have the relief I get, when I read Anais's poetry, or write it for you to read.

You can make it out of the darkness, I promise. Use the compass of light, and you will find your way. Just do me a favor. Never give up. If you are at that point. Call a friend, message your mom, drop a message to someone. People care, even when you don't believe they do. Soneone out there cares. Enjoy the read my friends. ~Richard White

<u>Concealing The Darkness</u>

Concealing Darkness

Darkness is real.
It makes me feel.
I try to heal,
but the wounds conceal.
I try to repeal,
but the darkness steals
everything from my heart.
The reality is unreal.
Nothing I can do,
the darkness is real.

Judgmental Critics

I peer into my darkness,
and it seems like I forever
doubt my fears, my dreams
and my heart.

I never dared to dream
like this before, I wonder will I
make it. Will I succeed in this
philosophical world with the critics?

Will they judge me, as they have
judged men before me?

My hesitation furnishes the fear,
and I begin to spasm with tremors.

Other people are here, I sense them
and feel their rippling souls near me.

Their presence calms me knowing even in
the darkness I am not alone.

Shadowed Mirror

I hate looking at
the repulsive darkness
I have become, chasing the
misery within my own
horrifying malice.
The shadows nauseate me,
and rip at my chest wall, wanting
to escape. I bury the hatred
of my repulsive being,
causing my own malignity.
Chasing any good from what was,
or what even could be. I am unable
to bear what I see, I find myself
intolerable, and loathe my soul.
It is why I shatter the glass of any mirror
I see, so I don't have to be reminded of
the disdain, and indifference I have become.

Broken Soul

My shattered soul
reaches for the darkness,
like an everlasting hatred,
that can't be denied.
It shatters like a broken bottle,
as it falls in disrepair to
the surface of pavement.
With a crash, it breaks violently
into small microscopic pieces never
to be reconstructed the same.
Demolishing my existence with
the harshest of venom. It cuts me
from the shards, as it falls to the ground.
Leaving me once again with an eternal
emptiness.

Eclipsing Shadow

My heart is covered by an eclipsing
shadow with a glooming sadness
of despair. The ecstasy of my bitter
unconsciousness disallowing me to
rise from the darkness. It envelopes
the true feelings I hide inside, guarding
and concealing the inner humanity.
I like it, and I grasp it allowing it to guard
me from feeling affection. The spitefulness
is bold but secure, and it holds me in the
shade of twilight where I belong for eternity.

The Darkness Awaits

The Darkness awaits Lingering,
between the shadows.
A constant recurrence
clinging to the fragments
of what is left of my emptiness.
Ingrained in my tenacious heart,
grasping to the scattered pieces.
Surviving only on the hopelessness
and gloom. It rages with a desire to
consume the corrupting battle in
which I fight, gasping for air, digesting
the negativity, awaiting that fatal attraction.
It torments my broken soul, gathering my
thoughts and absorbing the light I once knew.
Swallowing my happiness as the days roll by,
Crashing me into the darkness that awaits
Lingering in the hollow shadows.

Afraid of the Dark

I am not afraid of the dark
that comes at night, nor am I afraid
of the shadows that follow me home.

I am not even afraid of the dark
which you see inside a tunnel.

But...

I'm afraid of the dark
that spills through
the cracks
and crevices
of my splintered heart;
the emptiness that
floods through
my veins,
and the gloom
that fills my lungs
not allowing me to breathe.

Yes, I am afraid
of a unique Darkness,
one not seen, and
one that cannot be lit with a torch.

Darkness

It has no sound, no taste,
and is beyond your reach.
You may find it beyond the stars
and in the emptiness.
Clinging to you like a leech,
never letting go,
ends life and drowns your soul.
Keeping you from anything delightful
clutching your spirit like a demon
in the night, forcing your suffering
and driving you mad.

Cruelty and Crass

My inner demons are alive.
Some are of the present, and
some are of my past. They live
within me, in the seams of my
broken heart, breaking my soul
like shattered glass.

They appear from trap doors in
my memory, it has been happening
for almost a half a century.
They suck the life from my body,
leaving me in the misery of my
wretched Sadness, cruelty and crass.

I fight to stay awake, because
they can't find me here. Just
when I think I have them beaten
I crash. I knew my bliss
and happiness would never last.

The Monsters In My Head

I used to believe in monsters
under the bed.
But when I got older, I realized they
were in my head.
They have me clinging to life,
by just a single thread.
They frighten me more now than
ever, a feeling I will forever dread.
They have consumed me so much,
my eyes have turned to red.
Feeding on my sorrows and fear,
I want nothing more than to release them,
because they have been overfed.

"The Sky Is Grey"

The sky is grey, as I am every day.

It's like trying to do
Something you just can't do,
Maybe it's just that I am a fool.

I have come to the end,
There is an end to every road in life.
This means, I must
Take the rough road,
The rocky path,
Ya know the "one less traveled by."

Therefore, my differences count.
I am stuck on this rocky path,
and it seems I am on the better route.

I quote my favorite poem, because
I like the way it expresses feeling.
I'm not just a silhouette.
It's just that I use the poetry,
To find in me the symmetry.

The sky is grey, as I am every day.
Is it ironic, I say this twice this day?
You tell me, because I don't have
A price to pay.

I'm in the dark, with nowhere to park.

It seems to me, that I am alone,
And I wait for the call from god to set me free.

I can't seem to shake it loose,
These blues.

But maybe at the top of the gorge, the sun will barge
upon me, and become a part of me.

Is the sky grey, as I am everyday?

My Darkest Hours

I want you to understand my hurt.
The feeling I have around a crowd.
Can you be here for my darkest hours?
When the demons take my powers,
Will you hold me when my soul is broken?
and make me feel like I can be whole again.
I need to know you want to face my inner
demons, and protect me when I am unable.

I need you to know I am broken,
and I can love but not feel loved.
Can you see I am hurting?
Without me saying so.

Can you see my soul? Even though
I entangled it in the emptiness.
I want you to know my despair
and loneliness, and see I fight it.
Even if it looks as if I am defeated.

Will you clench me in your arms
when I am lost? and have no map
to find my way out of the hell
I inhabit.

Can you save me from myself?
Please I beg of you I need to know
you understand my hurt.

My Old Friend

I found my old friend.
just so we could talk again.
I saw it in my dreams.
The vivid photograph of
an emptiness I can grasp.
The pain I feel inside
Is returning, dramatically
Creeping. It encases
me deeper than it ever did
before, just when I was sleeping.
In these streets I walk alone,
in fear of no one listening.
So darkness once again
becomes my hallowed friend.

The Demon

I've slipped into the somber darkness
drowning in a jar of tincture, wanting more
I cannot escape it, it drowns me, asphyxiating
my soul, suffocating me. The beasts inside call
for it. Yet I try to push it away, but it continues to
call.

The demon needs a drink, it can't control the
emptiness. He has to be fed, but the bottle is dry.
I can no longer control him, The demon gets his
Revenge. Screaming, I need more, give me another
bottle, I scream for more; I am unnoticed, the demon
has become a beast and destroys all in its path, its
what it does, I can't control the oppression no longer.
I lash out in a rage, why can't they hear me, I need
another bottle; I need the taste; I need the hate, I
need the flavor, but most of all, I want my demon to
drown, it is only my drunken nature.

Taste of War

In the dead of night the nightmare begins.
It grasps my soul, and wanders me back to
an empty desert looking for peace I can no longer
find. Will I never return from this, will I always be
looking for the ghostly figures, look into their eyes,
yearning to be among them, I should never have
lived, I should have died there, I still taste the blood
and the mud, I smell the hot brass, and powder. I
taste the sandy grit, and I see their faces as vivid
dreams, like they are standing watch, or standing
before me. I hunger for them to stop; the desire is so
strong, yet when I fade to sleep they return. Haunting
me for a living, and grieving. I desire the night I sleep
peacefully, without the cloud of hell sweeping into my
mind as I drift off to sleep in a desert I never left
completely.

Glass of Rum

The air smells like stale liquor, a bottle I choke down.
I once loved the smell of a joint in town.
The smell of old cigars and mouthwatering martinis,
touched the end of my nose in a somber state of
mind, but now my eyes drift below my hat, my
shoulders decline, and I shake waiting for the door to
open and get my first glass of Rum. Just so I can be
numb.

Shaded and Jaded

Pitch black, coal black obsidian.
It's onyx and dark, its evil,
Its satanic, shaded and jaded.
Misty and gloom, it's a raven
after midnight, taking stable flight.
It is atramentous charcoal, murky melanoid.
A dusky fog in the moonlight. A rayless shadow
swooping over like a blanket, it covers, you and
chases you, follows you where ever you go.
It is caliginous, and cimmerian, all at once. It is my
dark shadow following me to depths of my despair.

Darkness is an Open Door

Darkness pulls me to
an open door, that
I cannot go through.

Light pulls me to
a closed door, that
I cannot go through.

One-day dark or light,
I will find a door
I can open
without a fight.

Or maybe...Just maybe...
for me there is no
door to look for.
Just an empty room.

"A Bottle of Fear"

The doors are closing in, and the walls of the rooms
are getting smaller.
I can feel myself in isolation, which drives me crazy, I
love to be alone, but I hate it also.
The shame of loneliness is drawn from my fear, I'm
not sure if I will survive it. For this time, it is a deeper
thought of rage and hate that brings me to a bottle
where I know that in isolation I am safe and as it
empties so does my soul.

Collision

The lights are getting dimmer,
my heart is getting thinner.

To be in a deep dark hole,
feels like something
ripping at my soul.

I feel I am falling, yet
I hear my maker calling.
It's time to go, though the time hasn't come this I
know.

What's inside of me I'm not sure?
Ignorance is what I am, and with it I can't get out of a
single jam.

I am alone, though my thoughts have grown to roam.
I'm torn inside, therefore I shall fall If we collide.

I shouldn't feel this way, and I have tried but
everything I have ever said and done has died.

Broken Glass

Shattered Glass

Ripped at the Seams

I am devastated and crushed.
Fragmented and destroyed
into pieces, some I still can't find.
The pain devours my heart, soul and mind.
Eating at me and pulverizing the thoughts I hide.
The pain dissolves me ripping me at the seams.
Splintering my dreams into broken shards.
I am shattered.

Am I broken

Searching for the answers
in the still of the night.
I ask myself, until I see
the morning light.
I don't sleep; the thoughts
keep coming, am I broken?
Please help me with this fight.
Can I sleep now? No I'm all right.
Keep going, don't look back.
I can't decide I'm about to crack.
Help me, Am I broken?
Just an hour nap.
No, ok have a good night,
I'll stay awake,
just for spite.
Help me, Am I broken?

Tattered

Tattered battered and beaten;
Scarred, bruised and bleeding.
I've tried to find freedom.
Yet with you I am defeated.
I want to love you more.
I can't find a good reason.
I can't believe you are leaving.
I trusted your words before.
This is the proof you are deceiving.
I am sadly mistreated.
I will love you nevermore.

Love is Blind

You punish me with your shattering eyes.
You leave me beaten, and traumatized.

I tried to love, but found only sadness.
What is profound; I only know the madness.

I can't get you out of my mind.
We all know that love is blind.

I should have known this from the start.
That you would shatter my broken heart.

You told me to forget you,
I didn't know love was something you outgrew.

I sit her thinking and look back at our troubled past,
and know, we could never last.

What Lies Within

My thoughts are pulverized,
blasted with dynamite.
Every time I close my eyes,
I think about that moment.
Looking around at the hell I am in,
soldiers lying in blood.
The sound of silence through gunfire.
Every thing is in slow motion,
bullets ripping us apart.
Shattering our hearts,
as another brother falls.
I'm crying; or is it the salt and sweat
running into my eyes?
At this moment I cannot tell.
I wish we were never here,
but we are, and the survivors of this hell
are broken, shattered, pulverized, forever.
Never to forget, never to forgive,
never to live without the damaged soul that lies
within.

I Can't Remember

I battle with the nightmare.
Crushing it and burying it down.
I hide in a bottle, I know
it's not who I used to be.
I am afraid to stop. I can't
remember who I was before
the damage and scars.
Hanging in and out of bars.
What was it like to go fishing with my uncle?
or walk to the store.
I am shaded and masked behind a cloud
of hatred, and fear. I'll just drink another beer.
What was it like? when I was small, mom.
I can't remember; the thoughts and memories are
now all gone. Help me remember, show me, please
I used to be better, but I can't remember.

Tango Down

Every time I turn the corner,
I hear it in a distance.
I see myself kneeling in the desert.
My body tenses, "Tango, Down!"
I hear my radio, and I confirm.
I close my eyes, I see the faces,
I can still remember the places.
I tense up again, and hear it all
once again, "Bravo, down I need a medic!"
He's my friend, "Medic!"
I open my eyes, and I'm in a different place,
"You ok, Baby, its me"
I jump startled, nothing to fear.
Yet still I hear, the distant scream.
I drift off again, and see it all again,
all of the places I have been.
Hands and heart go tense,
"Tango, Down!" I scream,
"Babe, are you OK?"
Voice is louder now,
"Wake up" she screams!!
I curl up at the edge of the bed,
sheets soaked with sweat, I'm in
a different place again.
"Are you ok?" She asks, frightened, I don't
Know what to say,
I've seen her face before
I've seen the fear before.
There are no more Tangos,
no threats, the ghosts are there,
following me in my head.
All I want is to lay in my bed, and get some rest.

Never Ending War

I'm locked away in confinement, isolation, and
silence.
Segregated from my past, I'm withdrawn, wasted,
and secluded.

The haunting voices in my troubled mind, I'm adrift
a storm of confusion.

The pain is sadness, maybe madness.
I can't decide or agree. The emptiness is over me
I want to become free. There is no freedom in
seclusion.

Or in my shattered soul, I'm at the bottom of a dark
spine chilling hole.

Screaming to come out, I shout to see if someone is
near. No one hears my tears.
They won't look at me, ashamed of my existence.
They mock me and chase me back to my fear.

I hate them and resent their remarks. It shatters me
and sends me back into the wasteland of darkness,
leaving another scar. It is a war, constantly living in
this dark mass.

Devil's Contract

My soul became the devils the minute I left.
I didn't give it away, nor did I sign in
blood. He ripped it right out of my chest.
Now the demons take control,
leaving me depressed.

I fight them throughout the day.
They always win, because there is hell to pay,
to the devil.
It is his sick and twisted screenplay.
His demons do his dirty work, driving all the good
inside away.

He will get my soul, that is a guarantee,
no matter how much good I do, he holds the key.
Once I took the first life, he became my master,
I will never be free.
That is what the devil said to me.

Shattered Into Shards

You judge me because of my scars.
Taunt me with the pain I feel.
What you don't know is every time you
do. It shatters me into shards,
particles of scrap, with no time to heal.

I'm left in a pile of pieces.
Anger and hate is all that releases.
You call me a friend,
however, it only seems you pretend.

You have no remorse,
ripping me down is your only course.
Shattering my hopes and dreams like it is
a sport.

Leaving me empty inside,
what did I do to make you decide?
It was ok to smash all of my pride.

Out of Control

I am knocked down from your demolishing
raze, like being destroyed with dynamite,
decimated and scattered upon the painful
ground.

Toppled over into a pile of shattered glass, and
descending into a ray of darkness no one knows.
A darkness so dark the demons are there, to toy
with my mind and soul.

Capsizing me, turning me inside and out, looking
for the weakness and powering my rage.
Leaving me to falter and release the demons,
that will annihilate my soul.
Their power grows more than I can control.

Falling Apart

Broken, busted, and cracked.
beaten, crippled, and crushed
defeated, depressed, and overpowered.
Abandoned, ignored and isolated.
Ruined, disabled and shot.
I am coming unglued and falling apart.
Subdued and shattered ready to burst.
Pulverized into fragments and shattered
into broken glass.

Breaking Walls

I am mangled, twisted and tangled.
forgotten and broken, sometimes I am
left unspoken.

I shouldn't be, I was on the mend.
I thought I might be around the bend.

Then you came and wrecked it all,
breaking down my battered brick wall.

I thought I could let you in,
then you left me broken in a tail spin.

I was wrong about you.
Once I let my guard down, you
played me for a fool.

I won't make this mistake again.
You are nothing more than bad poison.
Because of you, I have to be more
selective of my choices.

Shattered Glass

Compass of Light

My Compass

I have endured a lot of darkness in my life.
I never thought I could find the light.
But while in the darkness, I built a compass, a
compass of light, one that would navigate me in the
darkest of nights.

First I added the demons; I knew they were to the left
of me. Then the hell, and deceit to the right.
behind me was the darkness I turned my back upon.
In front of me was the glimmer of light.
True light eleven degrees to the left of the light;
sixteen degrees away from my soul.

With this compass, I can get back to the light. I know
I can find my way; but I need a map.
one without roads, yet rocky paths. So I can find my
way and make my own memorable footpath.

A conversation with a demon

You ask me how I got here,
but if I told you, I would have
nothing to fear.

You tell me you control me,
but I found my way out, and
back again.

I can't tell you how, especially now.
You would hide it from me, and then
I would have to find a new way.

It took so long before, you masked
my eyes, but I was able to overcome
and you thought you had me under your
thumb.

You talk like a friend; you think I
don't know who you are, you are the demon
that gave me these scars.

I can find my way again, you have no control,
and you don't have power over my soul.

New Path

I no longer worry, about my journey
at last, I have found a new path.

It is dark, but only sometimes.
I sometimes see a light, but it's not that bright.

I use a compass to find my way.
I know that I will get there someday.

Rise From the Darkness

As I rise from the darkness of my hell.
I have found a new place for my mind to dwell.
A world beyond my wildest dreams,
a place where the light beams.
I found myself here by fate.
leaving everything I hate.
It awakened me afore,
ending my internal war.
I thought it could never let go.
Although I am here in this new place.
Why? I will never know.
Its bright and green,
something I have never seen.
Something from a fairytale,
right down to every final detail.
Seems my mind is playing tricks.
somehow I need to get a grip.
I smell the air and now it is real
even though it seems, so surreal.

The Perfect Storm.

My life has been a meandering twist of fate,
just when things go great.
They shatter over and over,
and my depression begins to takeover.
I look for the light,
but it is never in sight.
I want to feel relief,
and not handle all of this grief.
It is always a confrontation,
causing me more and more frustration.
I can't escape it, it seems.
It rips me apart at the seams.
I pull to the light, clawing and digging.
The closer I get I feel it slipping
further away, every day.
like a sinking ship, ready to flip.
I need to know that there is an end
to this disastrous trend.
Show me the light I cannot see,
and guide me through all of this debris.
I need the light, I'm tired of the night.
It suffocates me, asphyxiating my soul.
Spinning me out of control.

Lighthouse

My depression is like a sailboat in the night.
Looking for the lighthouse, the beacon of hope
that I am close to the light.

But when I least expect it, I run into a storm, no
matter how bad it gets I stay at the helm.
Hanging on to everything, becoming overwhelmed.

As I think the storm is through, I see the light
burning true. I inch closer to the lighthouse. Yet, in
comes the storm once more.

This time ripping my sail, shredding any hope I might
prevail.

Grabbing my life vest as my vessel sinks out of sight.
I hang on to the thought I might make it to the light.

I swim for all I am worth, drowning in pain, I
somehow make it, almost insane.

I reached the light, but for how long? I am not so
sure I can stay this strong.

Returning from the Darkness

I am exhausted from all of this pain.
I took so long to find my way.
Now I am here, I have nothing to fear.
However, I am drained, wearied and worn.
my feelings all still torn.
I am trying to stay awake.
But I'm not sure how much more I can take.
I fought for so long to leave the darkness.
If I don't rest soon,
it will consume me again, regardless.
It took fifteen years to find the light.
treading through the night.
Everywhere I turned it was another fight.
But I am here I have nothing to fear.
Although just outside of this light, the
darkness is near.
I need to sleep.
Before I am pulled back in
I can't take these spins,
I can feel it coming again.
This isn't fair. I just got back.
the darkness just needs to cut me some slack.

F5

I can feel the rotation coming as my mind spins out of control. It can't be stopped, the dark clouds loom overhead, the thunder cracks, lightning then the thunder again. slipping into the darkness of the wall cloud, waiting for it to take over my soul.

I hear the sirens and the warning. My mind is going crazy now, no running, no safety or shelter, can save me. As the wind blows, it grabs my thoughts, my fears, my anger, hate, and love creating a debris cloud. I didn't want this storm; I tried to keep it on the inside, but it took over everything it's almost a mile wide. I need this storm to subside and let go of this F5 tornado.

God's Symphony

Flashes fill the sky.
An outburst of rage,
booming sound,
pelting hail
wind and rain.
Mother nature going insane.
She twists into a violent raid.
Grasping anything attached to land,
thunder clapping; It is nature's band.
Don't be afraid, this storm will soon fade.
More will come in her place,
wiping away your tears without a trace.
Sit with me and watch, it's the grandest stage.
Something sets the scene, look above, at the bluest
clouds you have ever seen.
Streaks of lightning filling the sky once more.
Listen to the thunder roar, gives me shivers all the
way to my core. Another storm for us to adore.
God's symphony, as he waves his arms. Mother
nature is the star of the show, with an eccentric glow.
Almost magic, an illusion as the storm comes to a
conclusion.

One Second

Just take a second to see,
the friendship you have with me.

And take a second to foresee,
a magical future with me.

Capture a second of time,
and know that you are sublime.

Grasp a second to know,
you are the reason to my rhyme.

One more second,
to know you are mine,
just one second in a lifetime.

Empty Park Bench

The empty park bench,
is a perfect place to sit
to be alone.
It is a perfect throne.
I don't want to be king.
Just be amazing.
I want to be remembered,
for not being conquered.
The bench where I now sit,
is near perfect I must admit.
Ruling my journey,
an expedition of abnormality.
A conqueror's voyage
for unfound knowledge.
The empty park bench
a perfect place to sit,
and ponder life's regrets.

Drive

Traveling down this road,
I come upon a challenging bend.
Not sure what to apprehend,
driving into the unknown.

Every curve a chance,
for something untried.
All you have to do is decide
not to be a victim of circumstance.

Changing lanes ahead.
A promise of freedom,
escaping the asylum.
Choosing independence instead.

Merging to the right.
Speed up to integrate.
You can't anticipate.
Just drive until you see the gas light.

Turmoil Within

The thoughts are uncertain,
not knowing what is behind the curtain.
The element of surprise is to precarious.
An unquiet mind, burdening to find peace.
An unhappy quarrel, within your own conscience.
Voices becoming obnoxious.
Driving you to madness.
All you feel is the sadness.
A melancholy of fear,
just wanting to disappear.
Grasping that last bit of hope,
like a frayed piece of rope.
Wanting to belong,
the passion to be strong.
Understanding that there is no desire left,
no self-worth, you are a disappointment at best.
Anxiety and depression settle in,
turmoil within.
You can't escape it,
feeling like a bottomless pit.
Overwhelmed and defeated,
like you have been cheated.
Alienated to loneliness, only less.
You open the curtain and see it all to be true.
you are just you.
It is the unfortunate straw that you drew.
Nothing can be done,
but gather your things and run.

Compass of Light

Here I am navigating to the light.
It is always a fight.
I'm in the darkness once more,
sailing to a deserted shore.
I try to leave the anxiety behind.
The demons always overtake my mind.
The light is near, nothing to fear.
The distance is aggravating and hard to bear.
Yet the desire to grasp the burning ember,
is so great; yet so far out of sight.
My heart winds up in a blender.
I am close. I just need to use this compass of light.

Voices

The voices I hear.
They only want to cheer,
and put me in tears.

The voices win,
putting me in a persuasive spin.
Every time, they get under my skin.

The voices rob me of being free.
Leaving me in a pile of debris.
Nothing left except injury.

The voices chant my name.
Playing this atrocious game.
Carrying on with no shame.

The voices scream in my head.
I'm hanging on with my last thread.
A strand of hope I'm not already dead.

The voices call driving me insane.
Leaving me hollow and drained.
I can't get them out of my brain.

The voices are delusional.
Irremovable
Like a crashing musical.

The voices are still.
Tranquil.
Please don't wake them.
It is finally peaceful.

Confined

The light is brighter.
Can you see it?
I can't decipher, if it is illuminating.
Am I hallucinating?
I can not be sure.
So insecure.
I want it to be real,
so that maybe I can feel.
I am so frustrated,
fueled with rage.
I have searched,
sick of being cursed.
I want the darkness to let me go.
Tired of being heartless, and low.
I am like this most of the time.
I need the light to be real, and it has to shine.
This hatred is not how I want to be defined.
Sick of being confined, feeling this pain.
Being burdened with chains.
Does it always have to rain?
I won't stop until I am certain,
that the darkness will not worsen.
I long to reach the light, need to fuel my fight.
Before it is out of sight.

A Stab at The Heart

I'm trapped in this world, I can't understand it; I think I am not even here.

What is it? It's not fear, and it's defiantly not a tear.

I'm ready to give up, after all I'm not asking for the world, just a little love.

What do I have to do, to have you here in my life? Do I have to stick my heart, broken to pieces, with a knife?

Shattered

Thousands of Pieces

Once again, I have been let down.
Fractured into thousands of pieces,
trampled into the ground.
For a million different reasons,
with that feeling of being drowned.
Fighting for air, praying to Jesus.
I hope that I will rebound.
From being attacked by my demons.

Shards of Anti-Matter

Sure, I have been flattered.
I have even been loved like it mattered.
Most of the time, I am madder than a hatter.
Because even when I love, I end up shattered.
I am flattered; you think I am a bastard.
The things you say leave me battered.
Although I put up with them, I am fractured.
Deep down, I know you are a biohazard.
Spewing your chatter, once again like it matters.
I cannot seem to shake you, even though I am
scattered, into millions of shards of anti-matter.
Then you are sweet, and my pieces become gathered.
For a moment I feel that word "Love" like it matters.
However, only for a while, because you leave me in a
drunken overwhelming stagger.
Once again I am torn.
Beat down and tattered.
Left in a pile, broken, and shattered.
You leave me there, like it doesn't even matter.
The pieces once again because of you are scattered.
Left for dust to plaster, once again like I don't even
matter.

Am I On Hold?

I am feeling destroyed like a pile of wreckage.
I look up for you and pray looking for direction.
But my prayers always go unanswered. Did my call to
you get transferred? Am I on hold for a lifetime? Or
just in this present paradigm. I keep reaching out and
singing praise, but I constantly end up ablaze. Like an
inferno that will not go out, I call for you again, this
time I shout. I beg you to just answer me, show me a
sign. That I am part of your grand design! You don't
even meet me halfway. Is it because I don't come see
you on Sunday?
So, I call out to you, oh lord; I need to be restored.
And not live in this mayhem and havoc. I hate having
to be dramatic, a life of constant disarray. I'm
reaching out to you every day. I bend at my knees and
pray. I guess I am still on hold;
and don't deserve the streets of gold.

Shattered Glass

There was a time when I was beaten, smashed, and
mangled into thousands of pieces like shattered glass.
Fractured into wreckage out of my control.
Abandoned, wrecked, and ruined. I couldn't even
salvage the fragments of my soul. I snapped and
everything detonated, exploding into even more
pieces of shattered glass. How do I sculpt myself
back together, from debris like that? When there is no
more beauty left, no dignity or glamor. I couldn't
even vision how I would look, without attraction. Cut
and disfigured, a body full of scars. Others watching
in laughter from afar.

Secluded from everything was my only hope at
survival, only to find myself in denial, and becoming
suicidal. I reached up for remorse, instead rose from
the ground. Out of the ashes and set on an
unexpected course.

And before I could say it, I was painted into a mosaic,
armored with steel, and shields to fight the darkness.
equipped with a weapon I could only harness.
So, when my demons attack, I can swing this dagger
and sword, and know that now I can fight, and settle
the score. I will claw myself out of this gore,
transformed, changed, and superior over my
darkness. Knowing what I stand for. A knight within
the shadows of hell fighting my way out. Conquering
my doubts and soaring out of this misery we call war.
Leading a crusade and growing more callous. Finding
a pleasant and reassuring balance.

Broken Trust

Yes, I was loyal I was even faithful.
But you betrayed us, choosing lust.
I am crushed that you broke our trust
Our love is now unstable.

Yes, I was honest. I was even modest.
But you lied, and you want me to decide
how I feel inside, but my hands are tied.
It would never happen again, you promised.

Yes, I gave you respect; I gave you my best
but you dishonored me, why is it so hard to see?
Our union, and our bond has nothing left.

It kills me you can't be trusted. My heart is
forever busted, all because you lusted.
You leave me disgusted; you tore down
everything we had constructed.
You tell me it's something you regret.
But this time, I cannot forgive or forget.

Can you repair a shattered soul?

When your heart has been so cold,
and you have a shattered soul.
Smashed into fragments,
like a grenade explosion.
Bringing you to the blackness,
destroying your emotions.
Like a never ending sadness.
Driving you to madness.
Permanently broken.
Eternally frozen.
A never ending malice.
Forcing you to lie there,
in a pile of bits.
Feeling like the abyss.
Emptiness in your mind,
finding no balance, with
a body so calloused.
Never really filling the hole.
Can you even repair a shattered soul?

Overcoming the Demons

Im slated and jaded.
Tired and worn.
Ive not fought a battle,
like this before.
Ive been around the demons,
but never like this.
This time I had to use my fists.
I broke the wall; I shattered the glass.
It all happened so fast.
I am free at long last.
I overcame the demons.
Drove them all away.
I just hope that now I fought them.
They can stay at bay.

Mangled to Pieces

I am wounded from your torture.
Disturbed at your existence, mangled
to pieces like shattered glass from your
torment.

You mistreat me and crucify my love.
persecuting our devotion into anguish.
you crucify my affection, creating a sadness
so excruciating that no one wants you.

I wish I never met you; you maim my
presence into a world of unknown.
You tell me you adore me,
and cherish my embrace. Yet once I get
close enough, you martyrize my words,
and brutalize the affection. Until it fades
into an unrecognizable universe.

I feel like I want you to go, yet can't
fathom being alone, I need you in my life,
but at what price? I can't take it anymore.
Your rage of violence will not control
my life.

Shattered Debris

I have demolished my heart so many times.
Its time I drew the line.

The endless feeling of being crushed,
ready to combust.

I can't take this pain anymore.
I am tired, tattered, and worn.

The agony of my defeat.
Living in pure misery.

Exertion from the torment,
determined to find revenge.

Smashing my soul into a million pieces.
Looking for a substantial reason.

Why I can't break beyond this point,
and show the world I too have a voice.

Forever longing to show I want to succeed,
but this shattering pain makes me believe.

I will always be in the darkness.
being held down, broken hearted.

Never breaking free,
always lying here in a pile of shattered debris.

Random Thoughts

Something You Should Know

I try to write words,
nothing comes out.
I just want to shout.
My head is spinning
out of control.
I need to tell you,
Its something
you should know.
I need you in my life.
I don't want you to go.
It's too late to tell you.
You're already gone.
It feels so wrong.
Why did you have to die?
Why couldn't we just cry?
Together we could have,
and ended it with a laugh.
Why death, why forever?
I don't know how to feel.
You're gone forever.
Out of my life.
It cuts like a knife.
So many thoughts.
I can't deal with the grief!
What were you thinking?
My head is still spinning.
It's hard to get out of bed.
Knowing that no matter,
what I do, in the end
you are dead.

Keep Fighting

Show me your scars.
I can heal them.
Show me your fears.
I can comfort them.
Show me you demons.
I will help you fight them.
Show me your hate.
I will teach you to love.
Show me despair.
I can show you hope.
No matter what you show me,
I will be there.
I've been where you have been.
I've fought how you are fighting.
I can show you what I have done.
It's a fight but your worth it.
Keep fighting.
The only thing I ask is,
stay alive long enough to win
the fight.

Cast Aside Once More

Neglected, rejected.
Cast aside once more.
Empty, forgotten,
alone again forevermore.
Deserted, forsaken.
Ripped in half
like never before.
I am shunned
Stunned, dumped again.
Left in the cold.
What do I even cry for?
When all you will do,
is once again walk out the door.
I know what is coming next.
My heart is hexed.
Your leaving me,
like an 86.
I've been nixed.
Discarded, outcast.
But I ask,
How long will this
abandonment last?

Goodbye (Suicide)

I am standing on the rooftops,
so I can broadcast the screams inside.
I need help. My addiction is against the wall.
Help me before I fall.
I'm bleeding again, like a waterfall.
The cuts are right this time.
I can feel it dripping down my wrist.
It's kind of sublime.
Come quickly, I have little time.
I'm fading. Kind of afraid.
I might die up here on this rooftop.
Fall to my death, I'm getting queasy.
Maybe it's time, I'll lay down now.
I guess this is goodbye.

Acceptance (Addiction)

There was a time I needed the high,
a substance to make me fly.
Today it's no longer needed.
I can feel the same without any shame.
Get high on life and not have any blame.
I can feel sedated with these rhymes.
It's not even a crime.
Doesn't even cost me a dime.
I just had to be strong.
Learn how to right all the wrong.
I didn't believe I could; I was too headstrong.
I learned to accept this disease.
Now I do it with ease.
I don't even have to think about it.
When I look back, it was easy to quit.
All I had to do was admit I had a problem,
and I found out I was awesome.

Felt That Way Before

Beat up, smashed up,
out of control.
I've used so much.
I can't take it no more.
I want a way out.
A place I can go,
where I will not feel it anymore.
That is how I felt until
I stopped using drugs.
I don't feel the way I did before.
Like an abused whore.
Today I feel good about myself.
The days look more promising.
Just glad I'm here, because death I fear.
I found peace with it all.
My hope is you can too,
before you fall.

Migraines

I wake up in pain.
I can feel the rain.
No, not another migraine.
I can't take it; it's insane.
Like it lives in my left brain.
That is rather profane,
to take over my brain.
I wish someone would explain.
These headaches need to refrain.
Happens every time it rains.
It like being insane in the membrane.
If you know what I am saying,
like crushed vertebrae.
It courses through my brain.
It's off the chains,
I can't do this anymore.
Please take away this pain.

Prayer in My Despair

Im seeking asylum,
in your silence.
I hate this noise.
It seems to destroy my thinking.
Makes me feel like drinking.
But 1000 are too many,
and one is never enough.
Staying sober is tough.
Can I find comfort here?
It's the only place I have no fear.
Feeling uncertain,
to give you my burdens.
Feel like a glass of bourbon?
No, I can't do that to you.
I'm sorry I am a fool.
What was I visualizing?
Like I was surmising an affair,
I thought we had a flare.
Yet you were only here.
To share prayer,
in my despair.

Devastated

I'm feeling jaded.
I want to be sedated.
Another day of being hated.
I woke up wanting to be elated.
Now my mind is serrated.
Another wave of being frustrated.
Feelings have been confiscated.
I'm devastated.
Hatred is elevated.
Almost like it was calculated.
I didn't know the bomb would be detonated.
You think I am fabricated.
I'm just isolated and illustrated.
Maybe a little intoxicated.
My mind is evacuated.
My heart is barricaded
behind a wall, like being incarcerated.
Like being suffocated.
They want me medicated.
I won't be manipulated.
I know I'm sophisticated,
but I am underestimated.
Sick of being humiliated.
I don't like being desecrated.
I just want to be appreciated.

Gloomy Night in October

I once had a hunger I could not feed.
A fixation I did not need.
The urge to alter my mind.
The addiction leaving me blind.
The high I could not find.
Almost loved the itch.
I hated the shakes and twitch.
Then came the shake and the ache.
I was ready to break.
I needed it more and more.
Until my friends found me on the floor.
They taught me; I had something to stand for.
I no longer needed to feed the itch.
No more burning the bridge.
I had to face the fact.
I needed to get off the heroin and smack.
I sweat it out for weeks on end.
Being watched over by some friends.
All over some bad breakup, with a girlfriend.
I'm finally straight.
In love with my soul mate.
Clean and sober,
since that dark and gloomy night in October.

Demons of Darkness

The demons of darkness must be near.
I can hear them in the night, start to cheer.
They want my soul, my pounding heart.
They don't know it's all torn apart.
When they come this time.
I will be ready, sword drawn in sublime.
The demons of darkness don't stand a chance.
For I am in a fierce warlike trance.
I have beaten them before.
They can no longer be ignored.
It is time they see I will be free.
The demons of darkness no longer know,
what I am about to bestow.
I have changed and no longer afraid.
This will be the last time I am betrayed.
I will not stop until the demons are all slayed.
Assassinated and exterminated!
I will fight until my end, even if I am condemned.
The demons of darkness will run.
I will take them out one-by-one.
It's no longer a battle; It is a war.
One I can lose nevermore.
I will not stop until I have spilled the demons'
blood upon the floor.

Where dark was the only light

For so many years,
I hid in fear.
My dreams were broken.
Bitterness spoken.
No one could hear my cries.
I just wanted to say my goodbyes.

I wander through the night,
where darkness is my only light.
Exploring my mind, trying to find
something good left in my heart.
Yet, the longer I look, it is all torn apart.

The pieces are spread here and wide.
I want the feelings to subside.
Bury them never to be found.
Constrained with no more sound.
I want to wander in the light,
hiding darkness from my sight.

Wash away all the pain.
Unlock these dreadful chains.
Break free from fear,
and dry my suffering tears.
Wander with peaceful bliss,
and leave behind the hollow abyss.

Misery

I am in Agony, discomfort and despair.
the tortured torment I belong to it
like darkness squalor, aching melancholy.
The unhappiness and desolation bring me sorrow,
like a suffering distress. I am a mess.
My hate causes of my own bane.
I am a burden on those around me,
like a plague of poison, pure misery.
The wretchedness makes me despicable.
Unrecognizable and cursed.
I chose this woe, and live with the catastrophe of
disaster and gloom. Like a heartbreaking tragedy
hopelessness in my own devastating misery.
The only way it will end, is the infliction of my own
fatality.

Wounds That Are Concealed

You may not be able to see my pain,
or know how I feel, just know that it
is very real. Some wounds cannot heal.
They just become concealed.
Hidden from your eyes, so you don't have
to see what is really going on with me.
If you only knew what I go through
every day. The chaos, disorder, confusion
and disarray.

I hide it all inside, almost like it is pleasant.
Feeling the rage and animosity. The hate and
anger is a commodity. In my head the
overflowing rampage is a passion, like
something I can't live without. Can't go
without. Like an addiction plaguing my mind.
Yet I wonder how I keep it confined.

I grasp at the hostility and malice. Finding
satisfaction in the bitterness and eruption
of emotions. Justifying the pain, like it is
acceptable. Telling myself that this is the way
I should live and feel. I know my subconscious
is telling me different, but I appeal.

You would think I like this pins and needles
sensation, but honestly it is more like frustration.
I want to be free of anxiety. I hate this
disability. This thing they call PTSD.

Suicide Attempt

Can you hear me now, lying here fighting for my last
breath? I bet you didn't think I had it in me.
I've been telling you for so long. I wanted to be free.
I wrote a letter this time; It doesn't matter most of
you didn't even see the signs. I shouted and I've
screamed. I couldn't take this life anymore; never
achieving my dreams. I tried, but all I ever think
about is how I want to die.
I listened to the psychiatrist, find the place that is the
quietist. I'm not sure that this is what she meant.
Leaned up against the bathroom door, the blood
running all over the floor. I wonder what you must
think; It's only been a matter of time. I've always been
on the brink. I'm looking down upon myself. I can
see the paramedics working; It's almost time for my
final farewell. Something inside tells me to stay,
something I can't explain, I want to go, I'm not even
afraid. But what is that telling me to fight, wait, I can
see the light, but it's getting darker and further away, I
can't escape.

The only thing I remember was slicing my wrists, and
feeling like I was being hit, then I woke up here, still
alive, I had been revived, but they don't understand,
all I ever wanted was just to die.

Just a random thought

Choose how you want your life to be. If you just sit
there, and not at least try, you will only succeed at
doing nothing. I know that sometimes things are not
always what they seem, and you end up believing
negativity around you, but see your dreams through.
Have faith, have the want to create. Dig down and
find whatever it is you want to believe in, and have
faith it is there for you to grasp, if you don't you will
always believe you are trash. But only because you
listened to those behind you, telling you you were. It
may be a lot of work, but decide what you want to do
with it. Are you going to work hard or just run and
hide? Never trying because someone out there said
your dreams were unreachable. We only have this one
life, you can't listen to those people, they are
replaceable, and you go out there, and making
something of yourself, even if it is unexplainable. Just
do it for you, for the ones you love, and for those that
love you in return. That is your only concern. So
when you get up tomorrow morning and look at
yourself in the mirror, tell yourself you want to
change, and turn the page. You decide that today.
You can walk away from the strays and choose once
and for all you are not afraid. That is all life should
revolve around, your faith, what you believe in. If you
can walk away, knowing you have faith in something,
you will achieve great things. Just don't wander this
world all lost. When you leave this world, know that
you fought hard in every regard. No matter the cost.

Spoken Word

Lying in Bed

I look back at the mistakes I've made.
I try to bend to my knees and prey.
But I can't seem to get these thoughts
out of my head.
They bother me so I can't get out of bed.
I want the whispers to stop.
They come at me like a vicious mob.
Anxiety and stress,
hit me before I'm even dressed.
The pain I feel is so distasteful, I just want to rest.
I'm living alone inside of myself.
Wishing I was like everyone else.
People tell me I'm exceptional.
But if I was, why do I feel this way.
Like every day will be dreadful.
I want to be helpful,
but everything I do becomes stressful.
People expected me to be somebody when I was a
kid, but I ended up chained to my own sin instead.
My friends all look at me like I'm a hero.
So why do I feel like I am nothing but a zero?
I have this demon inside of me.
The only thing I wish I could do is to be free.
I can't change that.
been there since I came back from combat.
I don't want sympathy, so don't give it.
I just want to belong.
I'm doing my best to stay strong.
I'm faced with negativity every day.
Like I'm always being betrayed.
I am reminded of all the reasons I hate myself.
I'm too proud to speak out and ask for help.

It doesn't work, anyway.
They tried before to medicate me,
it made feel like a detainee.
I felt worthless on that junk.
It was easier getting drunk.
Then I lose myself even more,
and all I can think about is that damn war.
So I can't go back to that hell,
I just come out of my shell.
People around me push me back there
to the places I don't want to be.
I just want people to see me for who I am.
and believe I am not a sham.
It's tearing me apart inside.
That's why I lock myself in my house and hide.
I don't want to listen to all the noise.
I've spent all these years just trying to avoid.
But the screams in my head leave me destroyed.
Because of this I live my life so empty.
There isn't a day that goes by that the devil doesn't
tempt me. I try not to give in,
but I can feel these demons crawling all over my skin.
I've tried reaching out to our savior,
and ask him for a favor.
But he doesn't get back with an answer.
Maybe I deserve this torture, what the hell have I
caused? for even God not to respond.
What did I do that was so wrong?
And live in this hell I've undergone.
Welcome to a day living inside my head.
Now you know why I can't get out of bed.
Living my life like I am condemned.

Group Session

I get nervous all the time.
I can't even explain to you why.
Most of the time I don't even know who I am.
I look at myself in the mirror and tell myself get with
the program.
The thoughts I have seem to always get out of hand,
most people just don't understand.
I hate my reality.
I had plans as a kid, what I wanted to be.
I thought I had a handle on my mind.
But I didn't I was blind.
It was masked by my pride.
Every waking moment is filled with dread.
I think about it, and realize that sometimes, I just
want to be dead.
There was a time when I tried.
I picked up a loaded gun.
But before I could pull the trigger, I realized that
Satan would have won.
Every waking hour depression knocks at my door.
I don't want to deal with it anymore.
I'm tired of this torture,
living in horror,
images engrained into my eyes,
hearing their cries.
The screams I hear I agonize.
I start with anxiety,
the depression attacks me.
I wake up so stressed out
believing I am a sellout.
I can't handle that pain.
Its like being hit by a train,

waking up feeling afraid.
I shouldn't feel that way I was a soldier.
I'm being weighted down with boulders,
set on fire to smolder.
Living my life that way isn't even kosher.
Yet people tell me every day,
if I keep going I will be OK,
but it's not OK to be like this.
I keep taking the hits, in sad remiss.
Facing the demons like a gutless coward,
left to submit overpowered.
Just when I want to submit and tap out,
there's someone there trying to hold me up.
Telling me not to give in to the sin.
They tell me to turn to Jesus.
All you have to do is ask, and he frees us.
I don't want to be saved, with all I've done.
I couldn't be loved by the father or the son.
So get off my back, I've taken my Prozac,
give me a week, and I'll be back.

Some conversations can change the world

Hey listen we need to talk. I know the things I say
you believe are a crock. But I want you to accept this
without getting pissed, you have a problem, we all do.
I'm not even saying I know you, but I've been where
you've been, I felt how you feel, look at me through
the mirror and see things just a little clearer, you don't
have to do this to yourself, just put the damn gun
back on the shelf. I can't tell you what to do, I know
that, but I know you want to live, that is a fact. I
know the pain gets real sometimes, and it hurts so
bad you want to be put out of your misery. I know
what you go through, it's not a mystery. It doesn't
solve the problem; it's not a solution; just look at the
others that have fallen. What have they proved? There
is a way around the suffering, in can be diffused.
There are so many like you out there recovering, full
of fear and doubt, so I beg you before you kill
yourself, please hear me out. I know the rage is
displeasing; When all the surrounding people are
happy, you are grieving. I know it's hard to find
people to confide in. Hell, most of them you can't
even trust, so I get it, it makes it easy to hold a
grudge. But I know people out there that are full of
love, so this feeling you feel is something you can get
rid of. I know you're living in a world of deceptive
guilt, but if you hang on just for a little longer, I know
you can be rebuilt. Stop living your life full of shame;
you know it is a game. You have to turn this around,
you can't always feel like you've been cheated,
hovering in fear like being defeated.

So right now, I need you to hang on, listen to me as I speak these words like a song. I know that right now you're listening to the devil's cheers, and you can't hold back the river of tears. I've told you a hundred times, I've been to this place drowning in fear. The devil tried to kill me when I was at my lowest, except I was able to be heroic, and realize the devil is my opponent. I found a way to try to reach you as a selfless poet. Please I am asking you, not to believe the lies that you are hearing inside. Wishing that you could die. I'm here and I've got your back, with my help you can get back on track. You can walk past all this clutter and be a lot tougher. You can subdue the confusion and demoralize your thoughts that give you this illusion. Think about all the people that love you; They are waiting there to help you through; I know this because I've been there. In the lonely halls of unjust hell, and I almost fell. But I promise you, take my hand, it can get better with time I swear. Just give me the gun, and I promise you, that happiness can come true, and if you can't do it for you, do it for me on the other side of this mirror, I can't get any clearer, I hope that I got through, because you may not know it, but I love you.

Finding peace

I can't take it no more, everything I was put here for.
I'm supposed to proud of myself, but I'm not, no
matter what you say. I hate what I did every damn
day. I went over there thinking the same as you; We
were attacked I just didn't know it had this kind of
impact. I can't tell you how much I still think about it;
It's been fifteen years, but feels like it was yesterday.
The army told me they were in disarray; we had to
show them a better way. But not like that, rat a tat tat.
Just can't go on like that. Everywhere in the world,
people living in fear. While a sadistic government
rants and cheers. There has to be a better way to
explore, I know we can't all be enjoying all this war. I
know even after I say this, a week later and I will be
ignored. Others out there have said the same thing.
But we continue to sink into an abyss of hate and lies,
no matter how hard a guy like me tries. There will
always be war, both on our streets and in the Middle
East. We don't stick with each other, the only time we
get along is when we kill each other. How do we look
under gods eyes, when we continue to kill a brother.
This is why I'm torn inside I can't look at another,
and tell him it's nothing to do with his color. What we
need to do is discover peace, and spread it into our
streets, and show the middle east we love them too.
No matter what they believe. This is my belief, I hope
that one day you can all agree.

Calling Me Dumb

They have called me this since I was young.
Always making me believe I am dumb.
When I am dumbfounded,
at the lack of intellect they possess.
I must confess, I am not perfect.
But I no longer accept
being called dumb, an idiot, or stupid.
Feeling wounded, like being battered.
Feeling shattered, from all the words you mutter.
Even under your breath, I know it is being said.
I already know how you feel, so just let it rest.
They have called me this from the time of youth.
But people don't realize I know the truth.
Because I am no fool, I have all the tools to rise
above the torment I endure. I will overcome the
obstacles and fulfill my dreams, even when all I want
to do is scream. You see my anger and my rage, but
deep down, it's the fuel I need every day. Giving me
the fuel to drive forward to make a better me, a
stronger me, and know that from the pieces you have
broken me into, I have built something stronger than
before. Something tenacious from the core, and I will
prove that, I will not take this from you or anyone,
anymore. Because I am not dumb, I know what I
want to become; I am not stupid, can't even be
disputed. I am not an idiot, and I mean what I say
period.

Memories on Replay

I can't take this pain anymore. I just want it to
subside.
I'm sick of fighting this war, it replays everyday.
It is a constant fray, a conflict I am unable to ignore.
I wonder if I would have just died. I wouldn't have it
replay in my mind, causing me to cry until my tears
are dry. It is like a 3D movie in my mind; I watch it
every night. I can't sleep because of the fright. I am
afraid of what more I will see on this DVD, the
cerebrum 4k ultra built in TV. Every time I close my
eyes, it's on like an award-winning reprise. On repeat
Forty-eight hours of defeat, battle and retreat.
This is why I hate this disorder. All it does is bring me
torture, locking me in, to deal with the horror.
I just want to be free like everyone else, and stop
hearing these mortar shells. I need to say my final
farewells, and let the ghosts of war, not haunt me
anymore. How do I do that, when I feel like I am
constantly attacked. I just want my old self back. Get
my life on track, but then, I go to sleep and there I
am, once again. Stuck in my Humvee, not able to
weep. So I lie there staring at the darkness, hating my
diagnosis.

EPILOGUE

As you read the book, I took you to the darkest of places. some so dark, you may feel you cannot return. I can promise you, you can return from that darkness. You can rebuild shattered glass. I may have taken you to the darkest of places, made you feel the worst of my pain, and let you see the shattered pieces to my soul and heart. I am here to tell you I am not in the darkness all the time. There are many times that my daughter and wife bring me out of that darkness and into some happiness. and those times are the best of life and what I cherish most. When I am in that darkness, I pull away, and deal with that darkness in my own way. I have always been able to find my way out, not sure if I drew myself a map and left a compass there for me to navigate myself out or not, but I always find my way back. sometimes, I enjoy the darkness, I could never explain that either. It felt good to be alone, and in the shards, I don't have to feel them, because the demons have taken all the feelings I have left inside of me. Although I know it is never a place to stay for long. If the demons find me in the darkness, I am unsure if I will recover. The last battle of darkness I fought after serving overseas nearly ended me. From my darkness, and pain, through poetry I hope it can lead you out of the darkness, and you shall find a portion of happiness you can live with, that doesn't always make you feel you are always alone, and always broken. It is how we rebuild the broken parts that define people like you and me, and how we succeed from those rebuilt pieces after you have overcome the sadness. I was once told that wandering around in your head alone was a dangerous place. However, most people don't understand why I wander alone up there. I choose not to take anyone with me when I go. I hope that this book of poetry will also serve as a map and your compass, anytime you feel that darkness overwhelming you, the feeling of being alone, and broken, or your soul is shattered, you will pick up this book and read not only the darkest side of me, but the side that has found the light, and made things a little less dark, when you find you can flick on a flashlight and navigate to the light, and find out that sometimes just sometimes you can come back from the darkness, no matter how far your demons take you.

As I stated at the beginning of this book, I have not had the inspiration to write poetry in such a long time. I felt now was the time to not only use the inspiration I got to write it, but I also wanted to share with you, my readers how darkness affects me. so, in conclusion, I hope you enjoyed this book of poetry, prose, quotes, and expressions from my darkest of memories, and deepest of sorrow, fear, and watch me navigate myself through the toughest of times in life, to find freedom from that darkness, and walk within the light.

About the Author

Richard White is an author, writer, bull rider, bronc rider, guitar player, poet, and a country boy. Besides writing, he also loves to hunt and fish. He grew up in a little town called Danby, VT. At 22 years old, he became a full-time professional bull rider and amateur bareback bronc rider. After retiring from the rodeo in 2008, he wrote and self-published his work. Since 2010 he has published poetry, rodeo stories, western shorts, and made Amazons top ten bestselling list in Sports and Rodeo category, and a top ten on Anxiety and Phobias with his newest title What Happened To Me. Richard loves writing, and designs his own book covers, and loves sharing his work with people that enjoy a good story.

He lives with his wife and daughter in Perth, NY. Where he mows lawns in the summer and writes during the winter. He enjoys hunting, fishing, camping and hiking. His other passion is being a firefighter and EMT in his community.

"Imagine all the people living for today"
~John Lennon

Other Books
By Richard White

Pages Full of Memories

Rodeo Dayz

What Happened To Me

www.ingramcontent.com/pod-product-compliance
Lightning Source LLC
Chambersburg PA
CBHW072149020426
42334CB00018B/1926